INVESTIGATING UFOs

A TARGET MYSTERY

INVESTIGATING
UFOs

One of the world's greatest unsolved mysteries
the story of the Unidentified Flying Object

LARRY KETTELKAMP

TARGET

First published in the U.S.A. by William Morrow and Co., Inc., 1971, and in Great Britain by Ronald Stacy, Ltd., 1972.

First published in this edition by
Universal-Tandem Publishing Co., Ltd, 1973
Second impression, 1974

Reprinted in 1976 by Tandem Publishing Ltd.

ISBN 0 426 11359 4

The author wishes to thank the following researchers for contributing material and offering helpful suggestions:

Dr. Robert Jahn, Professor of Aerospace Sciences, Princeton University, Princeton, New Jersey

Mr. Stuart Nixon, Executive Director, National Investigations Committee on Aerial Phenomena, Inc. (NICAP), Washington, D.C.

Mr. Richard Greenwell, Assistant Director, Aerial Phenomena Research Organization, Inc. (APRO), Tucson, Arizona

Dr. J. M. Holman, Manager Mission Analysis, RCA Space Laboratories, Princeton, New Jersey

Target Books are published by Tandem Publishing Ltd,
14 Gloucester Road, London SW7 4RD
A Howard & Wyndham Company

Printed in Great Britain by litho by The Anchor Press Ltd,
and bound by Wm Brendon & Son Ltd, both of Tiptree, Essex

Contents

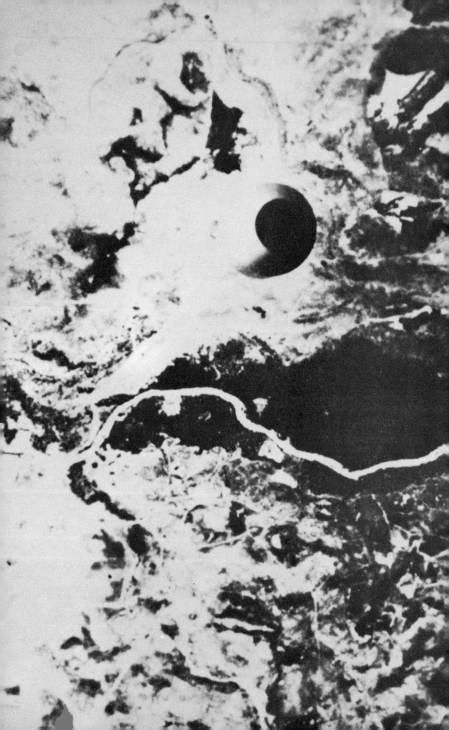

Introduction

In 1966 a nationwide Gallup poll questioned Americans about UFO's, or Unidentified Flying Objects. According to the poll, more than five million Americans have seen something they believe was a flying saucer. Almost half of all Americans believe that flying saucers are real, not imaginary. Thirty-four out of every hundred persons answered "yes" to the question, "Do you think there are people somewhat like ourselves living on other planets in the universe?"

When the poll was taken, it had been almost twenty years since the airplane pilot Kenneth Arnold had used the words, "A saucer skipped across water," to describe a formation of silvery discs he had seen in 1947. Between then and 1966 thousands of reports of similar flying saucers came to the United States from all over the world. The mysterious flying saucer gradually became so important that both government and civilians set up research groups to study it. Today almost every country in the world has been forced to consider the problem because of reports from its own citizens.

The question of UFO's has been a hard one to answer. The descriptions run the range from tiny lights flashing at a distance at night, to close-up sightings of discs hovering overhead, from stories of wingless craft moving and turning at incredible speeds, to startling reports of landings and meetings with space men or robots.

Certainly many people may see meteorites, weather balloons, or ordinary aircraft and believe they are seeing strange spaceships. Some make up hair-raising stories for fun. Nevertheless, reports come from dozens of people at one location, all of whom describe much the same thing, as well as from a single person. Men, women, children, farmers, housewives, teachers, scientists, and many others have turned in reports of UFO's. They are too widespread to be ignored.

However, the history of UFO's has been one of constant ridicule. People who supposed they were doing their duty by turning in a report to local police or the Air Force often have been accused of not recognizing a common object, seeing something imaginary, or playing a prank. For this reason, many people who have seen UFO's have *not* reported them at all. Doctor Allen Hynek, an astronomer who has given many lectures on this subject, always asks his audience two questions. The first is "How many of you have ever seen a UFO?" Usually about twenty or thirty out of every hundred people raise their hands. Then Hynek asks, "How many of you reported this to the Air Force?" Usually only two or three hands go up. So although thousands of UFO sightings have been made, apparently many of them never have been recorded.

Some people have compared the study of UFO's to that of meteorites. Not too long ago mankind was sure that nothing could fall down out of the sky. When people reported seeing stones drop from above, others laughed and called them fools. Finally in 1803 a great shower of meteorites fell on France. There were so many reports from reliable people that members of the French Academy of Sciences did go out to take a close look at what had landed. They decided that something indeed had fallen from the sky and made the first serious report describing a fall of meteorites. Over a period of time the idea was accepted gradually that material from space could come close enough to be pulled in by Earth's gravity. Only then did the study of meteorites really begin.

The UFO story is much the same. Before the 1950's hardly anyone took seriously reports that strange craft were in the skies. But gradually a few people became interested, and some research groups were set up to study the information available. Hardly any scientists were curious. Or if they were, they said there was no really good data to study. Doctor Allen Hynek, whose help was asked by the United States Air Force, felt there was little basis to the claims in the beginning. But over a period of years he found that many cases could not be explained away.

One of the problems is the very human fear of the unknown. Still, we have to admit that since we now are going slowly into space ourselves, others may be there ahead of us.

In the United Kingdom, hundreds of *SUN* readers wrote about UFO's. Half said they had seen one. In every 100 reported sightings, the tally was:

> **53 unusual lights in the sky.**
> **23 cigar-shaped objects.**
> **18 egg-shaped objects.**
> **6 flying saucers.**

Reproduced by courtesy of the SUN from an article about UFO's dated 21st February 1972.

UFO's Under Study

One of the factors in studying UFO's is government secrecy. Each branch of the armed forces and each government agency guards its own information. Something marked Top Secret can be seen by few people. Something marked Secret can be seen by a few more. Something marked Restricted can be seen by all people who have a security clearance. People who are outside of these categories do not know what information is available.

In this way the Air Force can control the public information about the study of UFO's. Officially the Air Force began studying UFO's in 1947. In 1948 a Top Secret report, which came to the conclusion that UFO's were interplanetary, was sent by Project Sign at the Air Technical Intelligence Center to the Air Force chief of staff, General Hoyt Vandenberg. Later the report was declassified and destroyed. In 1949 a Project Grudge report was released saying that all UFO reports were delusions and hoaxes. In 1951 a new study group was set up under Captain Edward Ruppelt. In 1952 the project was given the name, Blue Book.

The tiny Blue Book staff received so many UFO reports that in 1953 a special panel of top scientists was set up with the help of the Central Intelligence Agency. The panel was to try to decide if the evidence showed that UFO's were interplanetary vehicles or if they were a military or security problem. The conclusions were not made public. However, in 1956 Captain Ruppelt reported that the panel had recommended that tracking instruments should be set up all over the country and that the project should be staffed by trained scientists. In 1958, five years after the panel had met, the Air Force said that the panel had decided that the public should be told that there was no threat from hostile visitors. Still, over the years, Project Blue Book collected thousands of UFO reports, some of which could not be logically explained.

Meanwhile, two outstanding civilian agencies had come into being. The first, the Aerial Phenomena Research Organization, called APRO for short, was founded by James and Coral Lorenzen in 1952. It is staffed by educators and scientists from every field. There are about 4000 members, some from other countries as well as the United States. Many of them are in technical and scientific fields.

The second agency, the National Investigations Committee on Aerial Phenomena, or NICAP, was set up in 1956 under the direction of Major Donald Keyhoe. Its purpose was to continue the open and serious study of UFO reports. NICAP now has about 7000 members, including a unit in London, and calls upon teams of specially selected investigators to follow up many UFO reports. These two civilian agencies have worked continuously to give all UFO reports the serious attention they deserve. Because of their efforts, various scientists gradually have become interested in trying to solve the riddles that UFO's present.

In 1966 a research contract was given by the Air Force to the University of Colorado for a fifteen-month study of UFO's by a team of scientists. The team, called the Condon Committee, was free to examine cases in the Project Blue Book files or those passed on to them from civilian agencies. In 1969 the results of the study were published. However, there had been severe disagreements among members of the Colorado team. A memorandum in the files stated that the objective of the Colorado study would not be a full and open investigation, but rather ". . . the trick would be . . . to describe the project so that, to the public, it would appear a totally objective study, but to the scientific community would present the image of a group of nonbelievers trying their best to be objective but having almost zero expectation of finding a saucer." Two scientists on the project, Doctor David Saunders and Doctor Norman Levine, felt that the study was not objective. Eventually they were fired from the staff. Saunders then wrote a book called, *UFO's? Yes! Where the Condon Committee Went Wrong.*

Even before the report of the Condon Committee came out, Congress had set up special hearings on the UFO problem. A panel of interested scientists met and were questioned about their views by the House Science and Astronautics Committee. One of the panel members, Doctor James McDonald, an atmospheric physicist, said that since he had been studying UFO cases and interviewing witnesses, he felt that the best explanation was that some UFO's might be real objects or craft and that further serious study should be done.

A year after the Condon report came out, the Air Force's project Blue Book was dropped. Generally people thought that this action showed that there was nothing to UFO's after all. But many unusual reports continued to come in to the civilian agencies from all over the world. A second convention of scientists met in 1969 in Denver, Colorado, to discuss the problem. It was sponsored by the National Amateur Astronomers, and six scientists from various fields were invited, including Doctor Hynek and Doctor McDonald. Doctor Saunders, who had continued the study of UFO's on his own after leaving the Condon Committee, was also present. Again these scientists presented evidence that there was something very real at the core of the UFO problem. The question of the UFO's definitely has *not* been solved.

Above, UFO photo by New Mexico State University geology student taken March 12, 1967.

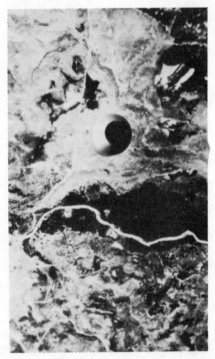

Left, aerial mining survey photo by Inake Oses taken February 13, 1966, over Guarico, Venezuela, showing similar object.

Paul Trent took these shots of a UFO at his farm near Mc-
Minnville, Oregon, in 1950.

Sightings and Cases

ASTRONOMERS' REPORTS

One sometimes comes across the statement that UFO's never are seen by astronomers. As a matter of fact, many astronomers *have* seen UFO's and have reported their observations. Here are a few examples:

1868 On June 8 at the Radcliffe Observatory in Oxford, observers reported seeing a luminous object that moved in the sky, stopped, changed directions several times, and then moved off.

1871 On August 29 the French astronomer, Trouvelet, saw several formations of objects. Some were triangular, some were round, and others appeared many-sided. He watched some of them hover. Something happened to one, which seemed to fall. It oscillated from side to side as it dropped.

1880 On August 20 Monsieur Trecul of the French Academy reported watching a whitish gold cigar-shaped object with pointed ends. Later he saw a smaller object leave the large one, making a trail of sparks.

1882 The Greenwich Observatory in England reported a "tremendous green disc." It had dark markings down the center, a mottled appearance, and a definite form with a dark center.

1883 On August 12 an astronomer named Bonilla made an unusual observation at the Observatory of Zacatecas, Mexico. He reported counting 143 circular objects crossing in front of the sun at an angle. The objects had streamers, or rays. The next day he looked again and the procession of discs was continuing. He took a photograph of one of the discs.

1884 On February 7 the Brussels Observatory reported a very bright light on the planet Venus. Nine days later it was seen to move out from the planet.

1892 On April 4 a large black disc slowly crossing the moon was watched by the Dutch astronomer Muller.

1894 On November 25 Professor Pickering and others at the Lowell Observatory saw a bright spot above a dark part of Mars. They estimated it was about twenty miles away from the planet.

1949 In August the astronomer Clyde Tombaugh, discoverer of the planet Pluto, made a UFO observation, which he reported later to NICAP in a signed statement. ". . . I happened to be looking at zenith, admiring the beautiful transparent sky of stars, when suddenly I spied a geometrical group of faint bluish-green rectangles of light similar to the Lubbock Lights. My wife and her mother were sitting in the yard with me, and they saw them also.

The group moved south-southeasterly, the individual rectangles became foreshortened, their space of formation smaller (at first about one degree across), and the intensity duller, fading from view at about thirty-five degrees above the horizon. Total time of visibility was about three seconds. I was too flabbergasted to count the number of rectangles of light or to note some other features I wondered about later. There was no sound. I have done thousands of hours of night watching, but never saw a sight so strange as this. The rectangles of light were of low luminosity; had there been a full moon in the sky, I am sure they would not have been visible."

1955 On November 1 a sighting was made by astronomer Frank Halstead. He and his wife were on a Union Pacific train about 100 miles west of Las Vegas. They watched a blimp-shaped object following a parallel range of mountains. It was estimated to be about 800 feet long. During the four or five minutes it paced the train, a disc-shaped object appeared suddenly in back of it. The disc seemed to be about 100 feet across. Both objects were shiny.

Photo taken in 1963 by an AVENA Airlines pilot flying between Barcelona and the international Maiquetia Airport in Venezuela. Note wing motor of plane at right and ground shadows of plane and UFO.

AIRPLANE PILOTS' REPORTS

Some of the most reliable reports of UFO's come from airplane pilots. Kenneth Arnold, whose description of nine shiny objects zigzagging in a line appeared in 1947, was a businessman and private pilot. Reports over the years also have come from commercial airline pilots and military pilots as well as crew members and passengers.

NICAP has made a listing of airplane-pilot sightings from 1944 to 1963, and it includes well over 100 incidents. One of them is the famous case of January 7, 1948, when Captain Thomas Mantell, an Air National Guard pilot, chased what he described as a huge metallic circular object. Observers on the ground had seen the object too, and Captain Mantell radioed that he was closing in on the UFO as he gained altitude. Then no more was heard. Later the remains of Mantell's airplane were found scattered on the ground.

1950 On March 20 Captain Jack Adams, a commercial airline pilot, and a crew member reported that a disc with apparent portholes flew above their airliner in an arc.

1950 On July 11 Lieutenant J. W. Martin and enlisted pilot R. E. Moore, of the United States Navy, sighted a domed circular UFO, which passed in front of two Navy planes. The sighting was confirmed by radar.

1951 On February 19 Captain Jack Bicknell and Radio Officer D. W. Merrifield, of East African Airways, observed a cigar-shaped object with vertical bands. The object hovered for a long time, then rose at high speed. Nine passengers also saw the object.

1952 On July 5 Captain John Baldwin and Captain George Robertson, along with two copilots flying for Conner Airlines, saw a "perfectly round disc" hovering above the Hanford atomic plant in Richlands, Washington.

1954 On May 14 Major Charles Scarborough of the United States Marine Corps saw sixteen UFO's in groups. The UFO's were chased by Marine jets, which could not catch them.

1954 On June 30 Captain James Howard and the crew flying for British Overseas Airways reported a large dark UFO with several small objects flying along with it. The UFO's paced the airliner, then disappeared as a jet interceptor flew in to check on them.

TRINDADE ISLAND SIGHTINGS

In the middle of the Atlantic Ocean between South America and Africa lies the small rocky island of Trindade. Once used as a military base during World War II, it was reopened in 1957 for special scientific studies during the International Geophysical Year. The Brazilian Navy built an oceanographic and meteorological station there for studies both under-water and in the air. Between November, 1957, and January, 1958, at least seven separate sightings of strange objects in the air were made by members of the scientific and military team.

Weather balloons were launched from the island frequently. They carried small radio transmitters, for signaling information about the atmosphere, and packages of instruments, which were dropped by parachute and recovered. During one of the balloon launches, the radio signals began to fade away strangely, even though the balloon was still in sight. At fourteen thousand feet the balloon was observed to be sucked suddenly into a cloud. Ten minutes later the balloon reappeared and began rising very fast. Its instrument load was gone. There was no parachute to be seen. Soon a silvery object was seen leaving the cloud. Commander Bacellar watched the object through a theodolite, an instrument for measuring horizontal and vertical angles. It was the color of polished aluminum, and the part that could be seen had the shape of a half-moon. It changed course as it moved. The missing instrument package never was found.

Another sighting occurred when an object flew very low over the island, moving toward the meteorological station at high speed. It hovered, took a zigzag course, and then disappeared rapidly toward the horizon. The observers said it looked like a polished and flattened ball with a large ring around the middle. The ring seemed to be rotating at high speed. There was no sound made, and there was a greenish glow around the object.

During a third sighting an object with the same appearance was photographed by a Navy telegrapher stationed at the island, using his box camera. The photograph showed the object with its ring. Later, on January 16, the Brazilian Navy ship *Almirante Saldanha* was getting ready to leave the island. One of the crew was Almiro Barauna, a professional photographer who had been taking underwater photographs. He happened to be on deck with his camera. Suddenly several of the men called to Barauna, pointing to a shiny object in the sky. It was moving toward the center of the island. First it passed behind a mountain peak, and then it reappeared, going back in the other direction. Within a short time it moved off into the distance. During this time Barauna managed to get four shots of the flying object.

Immediately Barauna and other crew members took the film to the ship's darkroom and developed the negatives. Although the images were slightly fuzzy, because of the speed of the object, it stood out clearly against the hazy clouds. A ring was seen around the middle. Prints of the photographs were given later to the Brazilian Navy, which had been investigating the sightings at the island. They showed the same kind of craft that had appeared in the Navy telegrapher's photograph. The pictures were analyzed by John Hopf, an aerial photographer working for APRO. In addition, APRO's Brazilian representative, the late Doctor Olavo Fontes, investigated the case thoroughly, interviewing the witnesses and the military officers who had been studying the incidents.

The sightings and photographs had been made by an unusual number of observers. The descriptions and photographs were consistent. Not only was the object (or objects) caught by cameras and observed

On February 21, 1958, photographer Almiro Barauna took this series of shots of a moving UFO from the deck of a Brazilian Navy ship near Trindade Island in the Atlantic. Small squares show enlargements of the object.

through the theodolite, but radio frequency signals differing from those of the balloons also had been picked up when the object was present. These sightings presented the kind of careful observation and thorough evidence that scientists are looking for. Unless we ignore the seven sightings, the five photographs, the radio signals, and other evidence, apparently the island of Trindade may have been observed by one or more very solid and real flying saucers during several months of the 1957 International Geophysical Year.

EXPLODING DISC OVER BRAZIL

During September of 1957 a newspaper writer placed in his column of a Rio de Janeiro newspaper a letter sent in by one of his readers. The writer of the letter said he had been fishing with some friends at the beach near Ubatuba. They had watched a flying disc approach the beach at an unbelievable speed. It looked as if it would crash into the ocean. But at the edge of the water it turned upward and began to climb rapidly. Suddenly the disc exploded into thousands of fiery fragments, which fell to the water. Although it was noontime, the falling fragments were extremely brilliant, looking like a fireworks display. A few of the pieces fell in shallow water close to the beach, and the fisherman and his friends picked up a large amount of the material. Some samples of the pieces were sent to the newspaper along with the letter.

Doctor Olavo Fontes, then Brazilian representative for APRO, contacted Ibrahim Sued, the newspaper columnist who had received the samples. They were three pieces of a very lightweight material that seemed to be some sort of metal. A powdery substance, which looked like the whitish powdered cinders on a piece of burned charcoal, coated them. The three fragments were turned over to Doctor Fontes, who took them to the Brazilian Mineral Production Laboratory for analysis. The pieces were found to be the metal magnesium of a very high degree of purity. The first tests did not show any impurities in the metal. APRO later sent a small piece to the United States Air Force. The metal was said to have been burned up in an attempt to make the necessary tests. The conclusion then was that the Brazilian tests, which had been repeated several times, showed that the metal was purer than the magnesium that could be produced by our technology in 1957.

During the Condon Committee project in 1967, Doctor Roy Craig, a chemist working on the team, arranged with APRO to make further tests on the samples. A Federal laboratory in Washington, D.C., made tests with a new method called Neutron Activation Analysis. The results were published in the Condon Committee report. The magnesium did have small amounts of other materials in it. One element, strontium, was present in the samples, and it is not found normally in present uses of magnesium. Also, when magnesium of high purity was produced at that time, it usually contained small amounts of certain other elements, such as calcium. No traces of these extra elements could be identified. The conclusion of the Condon Committee was that the tests did not prove that the metal came from a spaceship outside the Earth.

Then, in 1970, Doctor Walter Walker and Doctor Robert Johnson, APRO's two metallurgical consultants, completed a new evaluation of the Ubatuba samples. They found that the metal in the fragments was solidified in a special way with the grains running in a single direction. This composition makes the metal much stronger than it would be otherwise. Further tests also showed that the Ubatuba fragments actually were stronger in certain ways than earthly samples of magnesium. Studies of directional graining were not being made in 1957, when the fragments first were recovered. The latest evidence holds open the possibility that the fragments may have come from a craft that was not made on Earth.

UFO'S IN NEW HAMPSHIRE

Early in the morning of September 3, 1965, a young man named Norman Muscarello was trying to hitchhike toward his home in Exeter, New Hampshire. He was not having much luck and so was walking along the road. Near an open field between two houses something suddenly came out of the sky toward him. He later said it seemed as big as a house. It had pulsing red lights around some sort of rim. As it moved toward him, it wobbled and made no sound at all. Muscarello dropped flat on the shoulder of the road. The object backed off a bit and hovered over one of the houses. Muscarello managed to flag down a passing car and was driven to the Exeter police station.

Muscarello was extremely shaken as he reported what had happened to Officer Toland, who was on duty. In a few minutes, Patrolman Eugene Bertrand came inside the station to report that he had found a woman parked in a car about two miles out of Exeter. She was frightened and had told Bertrand that a huge object, which was silent, had followed her car all the way from Epping, a town twelve miles from Exeter. Both reports of an unusual low-flying object appeared to describe the same object.

Patrolman Bertrand drove Muscarello back to the field where he had seen the huge object. The night sky was clear. Bertrand and Muscarello walked through the field toward a corral, where some horses were kept. Suddenly the horses began to whinny and kick at the fence, and dogs in the neighborhood began to howl. From behind two pine trees rose a brilliant round object. It moved slowly and silently with a wobbling motion, like a leaf drifting from a tree. Brilliant red lights lighted up everything in sight. Bertrand and Muscarello both got back into the police cruiser and watched the thing from there.

Bertrand said later that the light was so bright he couldn't look directly at the object. It continued to wobble as it hovered, and pulsing red lights seemed to wink in a pattern from right to left, then from left to right. It moved away, sometimes turning suddenly, sometimes darting, then slowing down. At that moment Patrolman David Hunt drove up in his cruiser. Hunt watched it wobble and rock as it moved out across the trees, heading toward the town of Hampton.

Just after the object disappeared from view, a call came to Officer Toland back at the Exeter police station. It was from a night phone operator. She reported that a man had called her from an outdoor booth in Hampton. He was so excited he could hardly speak and told the operator that a flying saucer had come right at him. The police called nearby Pease Air Force Base to report the incident.

Saturday Review writer John Fuller became interested in the New Hampshire case. Beginning by making some phone calls to the police station, he wound up spending many weeks in the area interviewing those who had been involved. In the end he wrote a book called, *Incident at Exeter*. Fuller found the witnesses reliable and learned of many other people who either had seen the same saucer or something much like it.

Several men had run to a Hampton Coast Guard Station one night to report a strange craft that had passed over them. Mrs. Virginia Hale, a reporter for

Photo by James Lucci showing moon at left and glowing
UFO nearby. Questioned by Condon Committee investiga-
tors, the photo had been substantiated earlier by reporter
John Fuller.

a local newspaper and the UPI news service, had watched a large object from her kitchen window. It was evening and the object had appeared very bright. She was accustomed to the airplanes that often flew over the area. But this craft took a different path, and then stopped and hovered over a neighbor's house. She went out on the terrace to watch it. It was dome-shaped, but flat on the bottom. Its bright, bluish-green glow reminded her of neon lights, and it created a halo effect around the rim.

Mr. Fuller also came upon many unusual sightings near power lines in the area. Under certain weather conditions, or if the voltage is too high, an electrical glow called a "corona discharge" sometimes occurs around power lines. But these sightings seemed quite different.

Joseph Jalbert had seen a reddish-looking cigar-shaped object high over the power lines near his house. It hovered for several minutes, and a reddish-orange disc seemed to come from inside the larger object. In a slow zigzag fashion the disc dropped down until it was over the power lines, but still some distance away. Then it moved toward him along the power lines. It stopped just a few feet above the lines, and Joseph watched a silver pipe come down from the bottom of the disc to touch the lines for about a minute. Then the pipe was drawn back into the object, which returned quickly to the larger reddish object high above and seemed to disappear inside it. Jalbert's mother had watched a similar incident at another time about twenty miles away.

During the time Mr. Fuller was investigating the many New Hampshire sightings, seventy-three of which involved power lines, one of the biggest electric power failures in the country occurred in parts of the East. Lights stayed on in the Exeter area, but parts of Massachusetts, New Hampshire, Rhode Island, Connecticut, Vermont, New Jersey, New York, and Canada were blacked out completely. The investigation that followed the great blackout brought out that several UFO's had been reported at the time. A pilot named Weldon Ross was flying toward Hancock Field near Syracuse, New York. At almost the exact moment of the blackout he and his student pilot saw a huge and brilliant red ball over the power lines near the Clay power substation. They estimated it to be about 100 feet across.

At the same time Robert Walsh, a commissioner for the Federal Aviation Agency, reported that he also had seen a glowing red ball just a few miles south of Hancock Field. A whitish UFO and several red UFO's were described by others in the blackout area within only a few minutes after the power went off. In New York City Mrs. Sol Kaplan looked out the window after her TV and lights went off. She saw a large, circular, silver-looking dome moving up and down and sideways. She was able to see the shape clearly in her binoculars.

John Fuller felt that no adequate explanation ever was given for the massive power blackout. Some evidence existed that the power failure might in some way be connected with UFO sightings. Furthermore, at least a few of these UFO's had been observed so closely that they badly frightened the many people who saw them.

PATTERNS AND WAVES

UFO investigators have noted that at times reports have appeared in groups from certain areas of the globe. Such concentrations have come to be called waves. In the year 1897 a wave of UFO sightings occurred across parts of the United States over a period of several months. Another wave took place in Scandinavia in 1946. In 1947, 1950, and 1952 similar waves were observed mostly in the United States. During 1954 what could be called a global wave occurred. Starting in August witnesses reported UFO's in Germany, France, and other European countries. By October more reports were coming in from other areas. In November a wave of sightings in South America began. Some investigators have thought that the distribution of UFO incidents suggests a plan of surveillance by space beings. In addition, many sightings have occurred regularly over the world's military bases, suggesting that perhaps someone is looking us over very thoroughly.

Some of these UFO waves match very closely the times during which the planet Mars is nearest to the Earth. Mars is the next planet out from the sun, and because Mars moves around the sun at a different speed, the distance between it and the Earth varies over a cycle of twenty-six months. Thus, the two planets are in their closest position about every two years. In 1950, 1952, 1954, and 1956 Mars swung toward the Earth. At the same time the number of UFO reports increased. As a result, some feel that fast-moving Mars-based spaceships were visiting the Earth at these times when the distance was shorter and travel easier.

During the wave of 1954, sightings in France were so numerous that newspaper reports appeared all over that country. One of the most interesting was the clear description given by a businessman named Bernard Miserey, living in a town called Vernon about forty miles northeast of Paris.

On August 23 the night was clear and the moon was just rising. Monsieur Miserey noticed a pale light illuminating the town. It was coming from a huge cigar-shaped object hovering over a river a few hundred yards away. After a few minutes a flat disc with a halo of light dropped from the bottom of the cigar. It wobbled as it fell, then moved off at high speed. At intervals four other discs dropped down one by one with the same wobbling motion and moved off in various directions. The glow of the large cigar gradually faded into darkness. The operation had taken about forty-five minutes. Two policemen out on night rounds had seen the sight, and also an army engineer just outside the town.

On September 14 a similar cigar-shaped object released a shiny disc. It darted here and there, and then suddenly returned to the large object, which tilted and moved away. This event was watched in broad daylight by hundreds of witnesses in villages about 250 miles southwest of Paris. Other observations all over France described both metallic-looking discs and balls of light.

The French mathematician, Aime Michel, decided to analyze this information in a new way. Since so many sightings had occurred in France over a short period, he plotted all of the available ones on a map. He noticed that certain sightings fell along straight lines and that sometimes several lines intersected at one point. Michel called these patterns "orthoteny," from the Greek word *ortho*, which means *straight*.

Michel thought that some of the straight lines and intersections suggested planned flight patterns over the country. Other investigators have plotted sightings in other countries with similar results. Recently NICAP catalogued about 850 sightings in the United States from a wave in the summer of 1947. One of the investigators, Doctor David Saunders, discovered an orthotenic line that included some 36 sighting locations and stretched almost 3000 miles across the country. The orthotenic lines used by scientists actually follow the curve of the Earth's surface over long distances. Of course, the more sightings fall in a given line, the less likely the pattern is the result of chance.

Above, cigar-shaped object photographed over Peru by a farmer in 1952.

Right, UFO photographed in 1966 by business executive near Melbourne, Australia.

Other scientists have criticized the idea of orthoteny, saying that in any group of place locations on a map, some can be connected with straight lines and intersections. But certainly orthoteny and other statistical methods may become more useful in further study of UFO patterns.

ing on Route 3 through the White Mountains. The night was clear, and at that time of the year the road was practically deserted.

Betty had been looking at the moon and stars out of the car window as Barney drove. Suddenly she noticed a bright star, which seemed to be moving. Barney thought it was probably a satellite. As they drove along the object became brighter. They stopped the car several times and used Barney's binoculars to study the object. It seemed to be following them, keeping some distance to the side. Finally it was close enough so that through the binoculars Betty could see a large craft with a double row of windows. It made no sound and definitely was not a plane. Barney stopped the car for a third time and got out to look, leaving the engine running. The object looked like an enormous pancake hovering over some trees a short distance away.

Although he was frightened, Barney went across a field toward the object. Through the binoculars he could see the windows. The craft was tilted his way, and he could make out clearly perhaps six figures in the windows looking at him. They were dressed in dark uniforms. The craft descended silently, and Barney felt transfixed by the gaze of one of the figures. It seemed to be telling him not to leave, to stay where he was and not be afraid.

Suddenly Barney broke away and ran to the car. The Hills started to drive away. They could not see the mysterious disc, but sensed that it was still with them. Then the car seemed to vibrate with beeping sounds coming from the trunk. Barney and Betty felt a strange tingling sensation, and a drowsiness came over them. The next thing they knew, another group of beeping sounds roused them. When they finally found some landmarks, they realized that the car was about thirty-five miles farther south than before. Neither of them could remember what had happened in between. Both felt odd, but they could not explain why.

The Hills arrived home about two hours later than they had expected. They did not worry much about the delay at the time. Barney felt clammy. Betty took off the clothes she had been wearing and never wore them again. Barney had a strange itching and found a rash on his lower abdomen. He also noticed that the toes of his shoes had been scuffed badly, as if they had been dragged over something rough. Later Betty found round, shiny spots on the trunk of the car. The needle of their compass swung wildly when placed on one of the spots. Definitely something strange had happened to them. But all they could remember was seeing the UFO from a distance. Barney recalled the faces he had observed in the windows, but didn't want to talk about them.

About ten days later Betty Hill began to have vivid nightmares. She dreamed again and again that she and Barney had been taken aboard a flying saucer and given physical examinations. The beings on the saucer had tried to tell her not to be frightened. Betty was very disturbed by the dreams and finally wrote some of them down on paper.

Betty wanted to report the incident and called the Pease Air Force Base. She and Barney described what they could remember except that Barney did not mention the faces he had seen. He thought their presence was too fantastic to believe himself and didn't want to sound foolish. Betty wrote to Major Donald Keyhoe of NICAP, explaining the few details she could recall. Walter Webb, a staff member of the Hayden Planetarium and an advisor to NICAP, interviewed the Hills. Barney in particular was very reluctant to discuss their experience and wanted to forget the whole thing. But Betty felt they should tell what they knew. Later two engineers,

C. D. Jackson and Robert Hohman, also interviewed the Hills. Those who spoke to them were impressed with the Hills' sincerity and their cautiousness. While being questioned by Jackson and Hohman, the Hills and the interviewers finally realized that at least two hours of time could not be accounted for during the trip home. Both Barney and Betty had some sort of amnesia, a block of the memory, about part of the trip.

Not until 1963, two years after the episode, did Barney and Betty discover what had happened during those two lost hours. They had come to Doctor Benjamin Simon, a Boston psychiatrist, for help in solving problems that had appeared since the strange episode. Barney had become nervous and had trouble keeping his usual calm attitude about things. Betty still could not figure out her strange dreams. Although the Hills had retraveled the route of their trip many times, they still could not remember what had happened during the missing two hours.

Doctor Simon was a specialist in the use of hypnosis and used the technique in cases of amnesia. Under hypnosis a patient can be helped to relive past experiences that have been repressed or blocked for some reason. Doctor Simon hypnotized Barney and Betty separately over a series of sessions, which were recorded on tape. At the end of each session Betty and Barney were told that they would not remember yet what they had said. In this way Doctor Simon could collect material from each of them without having them discuss it.

What came out gradually through hypnosis was amazing. Both Barney and Betty described their experience in stories that almost matched in all details. They said they had come up to a roadblock after hearing the beeping sounds the first time. The figures standing at the roadblock had taken them aboard the disc, each one to a separate room. There they had been given physical examinations. They were able to understand what the beings were telling them, even though they could not really speak to them. Betty and Barney just *knew* what they were thinking. The beings looked fairly human, but had large eyes that reached quite far around to the sides of the head. There was no real nose and the mouth seemed to be a narrow slit without lip muscles.

The beings seemed surprised about a number of the differences between Barney and Betty. The Hills were a mixed couple: Barney was black and Betty was white. Barney had removable false teeth, and

Three sketches by Barney Hill.

Above left, impression of the leader drawn during hypnosis. Above right, second version of the leader was made later while listening to a recording of the session. Below, the UFO with figures at the window.

Betty did not. They tested the Hills in several ways. A device was clamped against Barney's abdomen, and it left the rash he found later. A needle was placed in Betty's navel, supposedly for a pregnancy test. She cried out because it hurt. Surprised, one of the beings passed a hand over her eyes, and the pain stopped. They did not seem to understand things about Earth people. Betty tried to explain about aging and how false teeth were sometimes needed as a person grew older. The beings seemed puzzled. Betty saw a wall map that apparently showed routes between stars. The beings explained that some were regular trade routes and others were exploratory routes.

After the examinations Barney and Betty were told that they would remember nothing of what had happened. The space beings apparently had used their own form of hypnotic suggestion. Only the later sessions with Doctor Simon had brought out the hidden part of their story.

Following some unfortunate publicity, the Hills contacted John Fuller, the author who had been investigating the New Hampshire UFO sightings. Fuller then presented the complete account of the experience, including sections of the actual tapes made by Doctor Simon, in his book called, *The Interrupted Journey*.

THE CANADIAN NURSES

An occupant sighting that took place on New Year's Day, 1970, was reported in *The APRO Bulletin*. The information came from two nurses working at the Cowichan District Hospital in British Columbia, Canada. Miss Doreen Kendall, a registered nurse, and Mrs. Frieda Wilson both turned in written statements.

At 5 A.M. the two nurses went into a four-bed ward to start the morning rounds. Mrs. Wilson took care of the patient who was near the door while Miss Kendall went to the patient beside the window. She pulled the drapes open and stood stunned by what she saw outside. There hovered a large sphere with a rim around it. On the rim were lights.

Miss Kendall estimated that the saucer was about sixty feet above the hospital patio and about the same distance from the window. Approximately fifty feet wide, it was tilted slightly toward Miss Kendall when she first saw it. Inside the cupola on top were two human-looking entities. Both seemed to be standing. One of them looked toward Miss Kendall, then touched the other, who was near an instrument panel. That man reached for a stick protruding from the floor. The saucer tilted further toward the window, and Miss Kendall could see the men from head to toe. One person's hand was visible, and it looked human and flesh colored. Both men wore dark clothing, and their faces were covered by some sort of headgear. The saucer then tipped away from the window, still hovering in the same location.

Miss Kendall called Mrs. Wilson over to the window to see the saucer. Both nurses then dashed to the nurse's station down the hall. The nurses there did not believe their story, but finally three of them went to the ward. By this time the craft was some distance away. Still, all the nurses in the ward could see the lights clearly. One nurse ran down the hall to a bathroom from where she could see the disc circle five or six times before taking off "like a streak." Later Miss Kendall said that she had been so curious that she did not feel afraid. She thought the disc might have been having some temporary mechanical trouble.

THE SCULLY REPORT

One of the strangest occupant accounts was reported in 1950. Frank Scully, a journalist, wrote the best-selling book, *Behind the Flying Saucers*, in that year. He relates that in the summer of 1949 he met a group of men working on magnetic research in the Mojave Desert. One of the men was considered a top specialist in this field. He had been employed by the United States government during World War II to develop antisubmarine and antimissile devices based on his research. Scully reports that this scientist, whom he does not name, described the finding of a grounded saucer on a high, rocky plateau east of Aztec, New Mexico. The investigating team found a damaged porthole, which may have caused the accident, and broke through it to get inside.

According to Scully, the charred bodies of sixteen crew members were found inside. They were perfectly proportioned and human looking, but only thirty-six to forty-two inches tall. Examined by doctors, they were said to be normal and had perfect teeth. The disc was disassembled and taken to a government laboratory for study. It had three rotating balls, which were some kind of stabilizers, underneath. Unfortunately, the control mechanism was taken apart when the sections of the disc were moved, and no one could figure out later how it had been operated. Scully stated that the disc had measured just short of 100 feet wide. All of the measurements turned out to be numbers that could be divided by nine. Some water aboard the craft had a thick, oily consistency. Interestingly, this same kind of water was described in an entirely separate saucer case from South America. In fact, our own scientists recently have published experiments with a special type of water that has these characteristics.

APRO also has a letter on file from a reputable physician who claims to have known of official government documents dealing with this case. However, there is no way now to check the authenticity of this report. If it did happen, no official information has been given out. Still, details of the description of this craft appeared later in other saucer stories as well as photographs. Are any of them true? Or are the later reports just stories based on earlier claims? There is no way of knowing, but the questions continue to puzzle the investigators.

The astronomer and mathematician, Doctor Jacques Vallee, has published an interesting listing of UFO landing reports from 1868 to 1968. There are about 900 cases, and nearly one third of them involve descriptions of occupants. Vallee does not try to evaluate the reports, but they are an important part of the history of UFO's, and they cannot be ignored.

CONTACTEES

A number of individuals claim to have met space people and to have taken a ride in a flying saucer. Daniel Fry wrote a book called, *The White Sands Incident*. Fry says he watched a saucer land near the White Sands Proving Grounds in New Mexico. He describes going aboard the craft and being given a ride to New York and back in only a few minutes. The craft was said to be robot controlled from a mother ship high above the Earth. According to Fry, the race of people to whom the ship belonged were descendants of an ancient and advanced Earth culture, returning to help in troubled times. The book includes technical explanations about the construction and propulsion of the saucer.

Another contactee, the late George Adamski, has written several books about meetings with people living on other planets in our solar system. He too claims to have taken rides into space on advanced craft. He describes cities on the far side of the moon and an advanced race of people living on the surface of Venus. In the books of Fry, Adamski, and other contactees, religious problems are of great importance. They emphasize the efforts of the space people to help the Earth people solve their problems of constant war and destruction. Usually they warn that those on Earth are not yet ready to join their more advanced space companions.

In the case of the Adamski books, our recent space flights and probes have given us information that does not agree with his descriptions. No space cities have been found on the other side of the moon, and Venus is much too hot to visit as he pictures it. Thus, the possibility that our neighboring planets support beings like ourselves is not likely.

One suggestion is that some flying saucers may be a form of projection developed by superior beings. The seemingly solid craft or even its occupants may be a sort of thought construction, which we sometimes can tune in on. Our own scientists have been able to use light beams to form three-dimensional pictures. Someday we shall be able to photograph and project images that we can walk around and view from different angles.

The contactee reports pose questions that are difficult to answer. Unfortunately, some contactees seem concerned primarily with the money they can make from lecturing about their trips and selling photographs. A further problem is that most claims of meetings with space people come from a single individual, so there is little verified evidence available.

Illusions, Pranks, and Hoaxes

Doctor Richard Youtz, a Columbia University psychologist, has an interesting theory on UFO's. He feels that many sightings may be what are called "afterimages." If a person stares at a very bright light source for a few seconds, and then closes his eyes or looks at a dark background, the eye will register the image of the light for a short time longer. Youtz gives an example of a case in which a pilot had been flying over the arc lights of a night football game. Later the pilot reported a saucer moving in the sky. Possibly the bright lights caused an after-image, which then was seen quickly against the background of the dark night sky.

As everyone knows, a sheet of glass that is dark on the back will reflect images like a mirror. If you are riding in a train or plane at night, and there are lights turned on inside the vehicle, you may see a reflection of one or more of the lights in a window as you look out into the darkness. If you don't notice the reflection, you may feel sure that the lighted objects are outside and moving along in the same direction as you are. Of course, if you are sitting still and the lights outside change course, then you can rule out inside reflections as the cause.

Faraway objects, such as the sun or moon, always seem to follow us as we ride in a car or train. This illusion, called parallax, occurs because we change position quickly in relation to the houses or trees nearby. They seem to be rushing past us almost as if we were standing still. However, the distant object remains at about the same angle to us. In the same way a bright star low in the sky may seem to be rushing along behind the trees and pacing a moving train at night. If you look out and see it, you may be convinced that it is a real flying saucer.

Of course, the illusion of parallax disappears when there are no nearby objects. Up in a plane the stars seem to hang in the sky. Even so, if the plane itself makes a turning maneuver, the stars apparently move. Pilots who have reported encounters with UFO's often have been accused of seeing Mars, Venus, or a bright star. But those who fly at night are familiar with the positions of the heavenly bodies. Indeed, they must recognize the sections of the night sky as part of nighttime navigation. Thus, the assumption that many pilots would be fooled by such optical illusions does not seem likely.

Doctor Donald Menzel, an astronomer who has studied illusions that can be mistaken for flying saucers, had an eerie experience when riding as a passenger on a plane at night. Those in the plane saw a light rush toward the plane at a fantastic speed. It seemed to stop some distance away and to move along with the plane. Suddenly it raced into the distance, only to return again and pace the plane.

As Doctor Menzel studied the amazing light, he

realized that it seemed to be flying low along the horizon. He also realized that a particular bright star would be just below the horizon in that direction at that time of night. The light from the star would be bent through a thick layer of air, making it visible, although it was already over the horizon. There were some mountains in the distance. As the plane moved along, the distant mountain peaks sometimes blocked the light from the star. Then the star would seem to streak toward the horizon and disappear. When the light reappeared, the star seemed to rush toward the plane. Because of its distance, the star gave the illusion of accompanying the plane.

Bright planets and stars, near the horizon, have been mistaken for UFO's in other cases too. Some colors are bent more than others when the light rays pass through thick atmosphere. Thus, instead of the familiar whitish or yellowish light of a star, a cluster of colors may appear. An observer could interpret them easily as an active UFO with pulsing colored lights.

Lights from the ground, too, have caused UFO reports. Searchlights, such as those from an airfield, can throw bright circles on low layers of clouds. From some distance away these circles can look like ovals or discs. The sweep of the searchlights can create the illusion of UFO's moving across the skies noiselessly at fantastic speeds.

Sometimes false images that shouldn't be there show up in films. In some cameras a lens reflection can occur, creating a bright image that looks something like a spinning top with points on both sides of a flat disc. At times these photographs have been labeled mistakenly as genuine saucers until carefully studied by those familiar with such tricks of the camera.

Unfortunately, photographs of flying saucers can be faked. One can sail a hat or a frisbee or a saucepan lid into the air and snap a picture with a fast shutter speed before it comes down. If the image is blurred, detecting the trick is that much harder. NICAP tells of an impressive-looking saucer photograph that had been taken by a young boy. The picture received local publicity, and the boy's family stood behind the story. NICAP analysts felt that the picture was not genuine, and a representative interviewed the family. Finally the boy admitted that he had taken a photograph of a model suspended by threads just for fun. In the beginning everyone believed the story he made up to go with it. After the publicity, he had been too embarrassed to tell the truth.

Fortunately, there are many ways in which photographs can be checked for accuracy. A double exposure—using two overlapping negatives to make a print—usually can be detected. In a photograph of a small model, the object close to the camera will not be in the same focus as the trees in the distance. An object that is actually close while appearing to be distant will show more contrast and detail than it should. Even movies of UFO's have to be questioned. After all, in a professional film like *2001: A Space Odyssey*, the whole story is told convincingly with models and special effects photographed frame by frame to show apparently full-sized vehicles maneuvering in space. Undoubtedly some of the same techniques can be used in ordinary home movies as well.

One of the ways the experts check a photograph is by trying to figure out a simple way to duplicate its appearance. If they can do so, the photograph loses some of its special importance. It still may be genuine, but one cannot be sure by looking at the photograph alone.

Often weather balloons have been mistaken for

FAKES AND ILLUSIONS

Above, photo by August Roberts of a saucer model covered with luminous paint, exposed to strong light and then placed in a dark room.

Below, photo of a steel mill in Hamilton, Ohio, showing UFO's created by light reflection between lenses of the camera.

Saucer imitations made with a Polaroid camera by Norman Vogel.

Above left, a penny on a sheet of glass as seen from below.
Above right, a piece of paper pasted on a picture window.
Below, a pot lid hung on a horizontal wire.

UFO's. These experimental balloons come in many sizes and shapes, and they drift for long periods of time at high altitudes. The sun reflecting off a balloon buffeted by the wind can produce a truly puzzling effect from a distance. In an unusual prank in 1966, some high-school students rigged up their own UFO balloons. They placed birthday candles in a framework of straws in the open end of a cleaner's clear plastic garment cover. The candles heated the air in the bag, which caused it to rise. Thirty of these balloons were sent up, producing a very mysterious batch of UFO's until the methods were explained. Such pranks have wasted many hours' time of serious investigators.

Several scientists have studied the idea that some UFO's are an ordinary but rare phenomenon called "ball lightning." Air that is highly charged electrically can form at times a loop or ball of current. The glowing plasma that results can hold itself together for a short time and actually move from place to place. Usually ball lightning occurs where there is other thunderstorm activity, but not always. Ball lightning has been seen to float along a field, to move along power lines, or even to float down a chimney, across the floor, and up the wall. Sometimes the balls disintegrate, and sometimes they explode loudly.

One airplane pilot flying through a storm saw ball lightning come into his cockpit, move toward the back of the plane, and explode. An electrical engineer named Phillip Klass has written about the effects of ball lightning. He feels that it fits the description of certain UFO reports. Furthermore, ball lightning possibly might cause some of the disturbances to automobile engines reported in UFO cases.

Sometimes a mirage also can create the illusion of a flying saucer. In this case a layer of warm air lies on the top of a layer of cool air, which is next to the ground. Light from a bright object passing through the warm air layer may be bent so that the source of the light seems to be in a different place from where it actually is located. Automobile headlights, for example, may appear to be two lights flying low in the sky.

Another example of a mirage is the sight of something in the distance appearing to float over a narrow band of clear air. Around mountain ranges complex waves of air of different temperatures can form. Such moving bands of air sometimes bend light so that the peaks of the mountains seem to be detached or un-dulating.

Artificial satellites, too, can be mistaken for flying saucers. Of course, if an observer watches a satellite for a long enough time, he can see that it is following a regular path. Special cameras all over the world are photographing the sky constantly to check satellite orbits. One would think that these cameras cover so much of the night sky that any strangely moving lights certainly would be seen and identified. But according to the head of the film evaluation group of the worldwide Smithsonian Network of Satellite Tracking cameras, the purpose of the sky search has been only to get information on satellites. If a light that shows on film does not fit a satellite orbit, nothing further is done about it. In fact, ten to fifteen out of every hundred light sources are *not* due to satellites. They are simply ignored.

Like light, radar beams can create mirages at times, producing a false image on the radar screen. But these mirages also occur near the horizon in most cases. Normally a radar blip is a good indication that there is something solid in the vicinity of the reflection. Again the argument has been made that the numerous radar stations would locate and identify any UFO's moving through the skies. But, like the satellite tracking cameras, radar stations are looking only for certain things.

Our Ballistic Missile Early Warning System, for example, is set up to follow objects with a trajectory like that of a bullet or a rocket. Anything moving in another sort of path is ignored. Doctor Allen Hynek reports that an average of 800 observations each month are rejected by our BMEWS radar scanning. They are called "uncorrelated targets," which means that nobody knows what they are. Thus, about 9600 radar targets each year are not studied. If even a small percentage of them could not be identified as ordinary objects, the time spent studying them would be worth the effort.

Of course, serious UFO researchers are not interested in those cases that turn out to be illusions, pranks, and hoaxes. They are interested only in the ones that cannot be explained in such ways. And there are hundreds of sightings whose causes are still a mystery.

Breaking the Space Barrier

One of the scientists at the Congressional Hearings on UFO's in 1968 was Doctor James Harder, a civil engineer from the University of California at Berkeley. He told of a UFO sighting by two California highway patrolmen the night of August 13, 1960. A consultant to APRO, Doctor Harder was one of those who interviewed the two patrolmen, making a tape recording of their statements.

Officers Scott and Carson were looking for a speeding motorcyclist east of Corning, California, when they saw what seemed to be a huge airliner dropping down from the sky. They jumped out of the car since they were sure it was going to crash. They heard no noise and thought that the engines were off. But when the object was only about 100 or 200 feet from the ground, it suddenly reversed at high speed. The two policemen were watching from a distance of about a half mile to a mile. They guessed that the object was about 150 feet long and 40 feet high.

The craft had a white glow around it with red lights at each end. At certain times five white lights could be seen between the red ones. They realized that it was no ordinary airplane and called the county sheriff's office asking for more cars. In addition, they asked the office to contact a nearby radar base. By telephone the radar base said that they had picked up the object on radar, but did not know what it was.

The craft moved toward the two policemen, coming lower to within about 150 yards. It performed many strange maneuvers, hovering, moving slowly in various directions, moving at high speeds, and reversing directions without stopping. As the object began to move away the policemen followed it in their car for about two hours. They felt it was aware of them. It seemed to be playing hide-and-seek, usually staying perhaps a half mile away.

UFO PROPULSION

Doctor Harder explained that the California sighting was typical of those in which the unusual flight abilities of UFO's have been observed. The objects often make little or no sound, can hover, move slowly or accelerate at rapid speeds, and make right-angle turns or reverse directions with amazing sharpness.

Many reports have described the slow movements of UFO's as a wobbling motion, often comparing it to that of a falling leaf or a boat floating in the water. The fast turns seem to defy the laws of inertia. Inertia is the effective force that tends to keep an object going in the direction in which it is moving already. The faster it is traveling and the heavier it is, the harder it is to change course. Thus, our fast-moving jets make long sweeping loops, taking miles of sky to turn around. Inertia also is the reason why the people inside a vehicle tend to keep moving in a straight line as the vehicle itself turns.

If UFO's are aircraft that work like ours, they could not maneuver the way they do. But the "falling-leaf" motion that has been reported in some cases may be an important clue to the mystery. A leaf falls as it does because it has so little mass for its size. The gravitational force is slight while the broad surface of the leaf presses against the air like a cushion as it falls, swinging a little from side to side like a pendulum. Each time it tilts slightly, air spills over the edge. Some UFO's perform in a partly similar way.

Another clue can be found in the antics of a tiny insect called the hover fly. It has so little mass that the forces from its rapidly fluttering wings can be much greater than its weight. It can hover motionless, drift slowly, move easily up or down, back and forth, and from side to side. The movements can be so fast that the fly seems to vanish from one spot and reappear hovering motionless several feet away. It can change speed or direction almost instantaneously. Again these characteristics seem to be typical of certain UFO's.

The one thing the leaf and the fly have in common is low mass. Thus, if the mass of a large craft and its contents somehow could be reduced enough, it too might accomplish the "impossible" things that some UFO's seem to do.

Doctor Harder lists a second UFO report that also includes helpful information about UFO flight. The sighting was made by a chemist named Wells Allan Webb on May 5, 1953. At about 10 o'clock in the morning he was approximately seven miles north of Yuma, Arizona, near Spain Flying Field. First he noticed some low-flying jets. Next he saw a small white object in a clear sky. It looked oblong as it traveled east. Then it seemed circular, and Webb saw a series of dark rings around it. The outer ring was about six times as wide as the white disc itself, and there were light spaces between the dark rings.

Mr. Webb happened to be wearing Polaroid glasses. When he took them off and looked at the object, the dark rings had disappeared. When he put the glasses back on, the rings were there. Something around the object was rotating light in various ways, so that some of it passed through Mr. Webb's Polaroid glasses and some did not.

Doctor Harder, when he examined Mr. Webb's

report, realized that such polarization of light would occur where there was a very strong electromagnetic field. The sighting with the Polaroid glasses is evidence that the disc was surrounded by such a field.

Another observation that turns up in certain reports is that the saucer rotates. Sometimes the entire machine is spinning like a top. Sometimes the rim section of a disc seems to rotate. Other reports describe a rotating ring located either above or below the rim, while the rest of the craft remains still.

Such a sighting was made by George Pedley on January 19, 1966. Pedley was driving a tractor near Horseshoe Lagoon, a swamp in Queensland, Australia. He heard a loud hissing sound like air leaking from a tire, and a blue-gray machine rose from the swamp about twenty-five yards away. It looked about twenty-five feet wide and nine feet high. It was spinning as it climbed, and then moved off at "terrific speed."

Newspaper reporter Ben Davie investigated Pedley's report. In the swamp area where the saucer had been seen there was a large circle made by grass that had been torn up by the roots. Davie found that other residents had observed similar saucers before Pedley's report. In addition, a number of flattened

Photo of one of several circles of flattened grass found following UFO reports during 1966 in Tully, Queensland, Australia.

circles had been found in the grasslands. Davie inspected five of them. Each was a perfect circle of dead grass surrounded by green grass that was still growing. There was no sign of heat or scorching. The grass in four of the "nests" had been flattened in a clockwise direction. In one circle it was flattened in a counter-clockwise direction.

ELECTRICAL EFFECTS

Many reports that involve a saucer seen close to a moving car state that it has had a strange effect on the car. One such instance was described by Jerry Simons, a forester who was camping out at Split Rock Pond, south of Newfoundland, New Jersey.

Simons was driving north in his car and noticed a red glow in the rearview mirror. At first he thought his brake light was stuck, but the glow became brighter. At last Simons stopped his car and leaned out the open window to get a better look behind him. What had seemed at first like a glowing light now appeared to be a solid body just behind and above him. Simons guessed that it was twenty-five or thirty feet wide, and five or six feet high. He drove away, but the object followed him.

Suddenly all the electrical equipment in the car stopped working: the headlights, dashlights, and the engine ignition. As the object fell farther behind, the electrical system returned to normal and Simons moved on. During the drive the electrical system failed three times, when the object came close. When it lagged behind or moved to one side, everything began working again. Light from the object threw a glow all around the car.

The UFO followed Simons for about ten minutes until he reached Newfoundland. He told the hair-raising story to Thomas Byrnes, Superintendent of the Newark Water Shed in Newfoundland. Doctor Berthold Schwarz, a Montclair Hospital psychiatrist and member of both NICAP and APRO, investigated the case and published the account in *Medical Times*, because of the unusual aftereffects of the incident.

When Simons parked his car at the reservoir office, he turned off his motor. When he came out again, the motor was on. The car was examined later, but there was no explanation. Then unexplainably, after just a few weeks, the engine suddenly blew up while Simons was driving.

Also a strange physical illness bothered Simons

for about six months. Every month for three or four days he became ill with fatigue, soreness, muscular weakness, and chills. The recurring sickness caused Simons to lose thirty-five pounds before he gradually recovered, and its exact cause never was identified. One guess is that the electrical field of the UFO disturbed Simons' body just as it strangely affected the electrical system of his car.

GRAVITY

Electromagnetic effects have been described in many UFO reports, and some investigators feel that they are caused by the propulsion system of the craft. In some ways we are using electromagnetic principles to propel our own spacecraft. Our first space engines have been rockets in which fuel is burned and hot gases are ejected, thrusting the rocket forward. Now plasma propulsion systems are being developed for longer space flights.

Professor Robert Jahn and others at Princeton University's Guggenheim Propulsion Laboratories have done new research on plasma propulsion. They speed up molecules of electrified, or ionized, gases electromagnetically as they are ejected from the engine. By increasing the speed of the ejected gases they hope to enable the spacecraft to reach very high speeds. In other future engines, light will be ejected, causing the rocket to gain speeds closer to that of light itself. However, these great speeds will be achieved only in deep space, where the rocket is relatively free of gravity.

Admittedly occasional UFO reports describe flames shooting out of a craft, or a disc taking off with a blast and a roar, scorching the ground. But in most cases flying saucers, even when observed closely, are said to have a humming sound or no sound at all. A glow like that of ionized gas may be seen around a metallic disc, or the entire disc may seem to change glowing colors as it changes speed. These characteristics are not at all like those of the craft we are sending into space presently.

In order to explain the behavior of some flying saucers we have to suppose that there is a gravity control that we do not know about. Many will argue that flying saucers cannot be real for this reason. They say that such craft do not operate according to the basic laws of physics. But the history of science shows that new principles appear again and again. Certainly if mass could be controlled or reduced, much that has been noted about saucers could be explained without violating the laws of physics that we know today.

LIFE ON OTHER WORLDS

The idea of finding life on other worlds always has fascinated people. It is both exciting and, at first, somewhat frightening. Much speculation has centered around the possibility of life on other planets in our own solar system. When there was little exact information about these planets, one could imagine almost anything. But gradually our space program has filled in our knowledge, starting with the planets closest to us. We have landed on the moon, and Mars has been visited with fly-by probes. Instrument packages have been parachuted into the atmosphere of Venus.

Now we know these places are far different from the Earth. Our moon has no atmosphere, and the temperatures are so extreme that one must move about in a space suit. Mars has an even thinner atmosphere than the astronomers had guessed. Possibilities of animal or plant life there are not ruled out, but the conditions are vastly different from those on Earth. Venus has an extremely thick atmosphere, made up of gases that we could not breathe. The parachute probes have indicated that it may be as hot as 700 degrees near the surface, because the heat is trapped by the heavy atmosphere.

Mercury, closest to the sun, may be almost as hot as Venus on the light side or several hundred degrees below on the dark side. Jupiter is so massive that it is practically a star, producing its own radiation. Both Jupiter and Saturn have atmospheres that would be poisonous to beings adapted to that of the present Earth. Little is known about conditions on Uranus, Neptune, or Pluto, but because they receive less radiation from the sun, scientists suppose that they are very cold.

Interestingly, despite the variation in size among the planets, the pull of gravity varies less than one might think. The large planets—Saturn, Neptune, or Uranus—are not as dense, so the amount of pull is not much more than that on Earth. Thus, we would not weigh very much more than we do here on Earth. Venus is only slightly smaller than Earth, and we would weigh only slightly less there. On Mars we would weigh about one third as much, and on our moon about one fifth as much. Only massive Jupiter would present a problem. There we would weigh more than twice what we do here. On the other planets we could move about with relative ease. The difficulty in adapting human life to conditions on the planets, therefore, seems to be the different atmospheres and the extreme temperatures.

Of course, conditions on Earth have their own extremes. As a result, life on Earth covers an amazing variety from tiny viruses that can exist in the cold of space to the species that live underwater. We are finding that the dolphin has an advanced brain like ours, patterns of speech, and other indications of a high level of intelligence. Who can guess what forms intelligence may take elsewhere?

Biologists say that life on other planets is probably based on carbon atoms like life on our planet. For this reason the development elsewhere of beings that we could call humanoids seems likely. They might not look like us, but would probably have the same number of arms and legs, eyes and ears, and other body parts. Still, life also might be built out of other chains of elements besides carbon, such as silicon, and it could turn out differently.

Another consideration is that life elsewhere does not have to be on the surface of planets. We are used to the idea of ocean cruisers that stop at scattered islands. People live on board the cruisers. Occasionally a cruiser has to stay in port for repairs, but most of the time it is in transit. Any civilization with a lot of experience in space travel will be able to do the same and more. We ourselves have plans for constructing orbiting platforms in space. Within a relatively short time we will be roaming space with large "living units" having many of the comforts of home. One can imagine giant space cities that need no single planet as home. Contact with planets would be made only for trade purposes, for communication, or for exploration.

Some have said that distances to other stars are too great for travel through deep space. But building craft that will approach the speed of light over long distances probably will be possible. In addition, we are studying methods of hibernation, so that perhaps space travelers can be supercooled or even frozen, and then warmed up at the end of the trip to resume activity. Many believe that nothing can go faster than the speed of light. But suppose we could pass the speed of light? Perhaps one day this barrier will be broken just as other obstacles have disappeared with new discoveries.

Another way of breaking the space barrier is being explored by scientists in many countries. The study of extrasensory perception has shown that accurate information sometimes can be perceived over great distances without using any normal means of communication. Apparently this information travels from mind to mind. In other cases, a person who is resting feels a part of himself transported to a distant location and can see accurately what is happening there. Thus, it may be possible to project mentally to another planet with a chance to make observations as carefully as if one were actually there. It has been suggested that some UFO's seen by earth observers may be highly developed mental projections produced by superior beings located elsewhere. Too little is known to rule out these possibilities.

Astronomers tell us that our visible universe is probably full of stars that have families of planets. The chances are excellent that on many of them beings like ourselves could live comfortably. The universe may be swarming with beings much like ourselves, some in early stages of development, some about as far along as we are, and others so far ahead that their styles of travel and existence would seem almost unbelievable. Of course, those races that are most advanced will have mastered the arts of space travel.

In any case, advanced races would probably explore us or visit us on their own terms, perhaps in ways we would find hard to understand until our own development reached certain stages. Many UFO reports indicate that such visitors may have been here already. This exciting possibility is what makes the study of UFO's so important and so fascinating.

UFO SOCIETIES AND PUBLICATIONS

The following list is a selection of the more serious societies and publications dedicated to solving the UFO enigma. This list is far from complete and it is worth remarking that there are 20 or more local groups and societies in the United Kingdom alone, many of whom produce their own journal or newsletter. Some societies have varying subscription arrangements, and these often include membership with additional benefits. Full details should be obtained direct from the organisation (enclose an international reply coupon if writing abroad) and some publishers will supply a free sample copy on request.

Australia

U.F.O. Investigation Centre
(UFOIC)
P.O. Box E170
St. James
Sydney, 2000

Publication:
UFOIC NEWSLETTER and
AUSTRALIAN UFO REVIEW

Victorian U.F.O. Research Society
P.O. Box 43
Moorabbin
3189, Victoria

Publication: AUSTRALIAN UFO
BULLETIN and AUSTRALIAN
FLYING SAUCER REVIEW

Belgium

Societe Belge d'Etude des
Phenomenes Spatiaux (SOBEPS)
Boulevard Aristide Briand, 26
1070 Brussels

Publication: INFORESPACE

Denmark

Skandinavisk UFO Information
(SUFOI) (Founded 1957)
Ingstrup Alle 35
2770 Kastrup

Publication: UFO-NYT

Finland

Interplanetisit ry—
Interplanetisterna rf
Postilokero 10101
Helsinki 10

Publication: VIMANA

France

Groupe D'Etudes des Objets
Spatiaux de France (GEOS)
77 Saint-Denis les Rebais

Publication:
LES EXTRATERRESTRES

Groupment d'Etude de Phenomenes
Aeriens et d'Objets Spatiaux
Insolites (GEPA)
69 Rue de la Tombe-Issoire
Paris 14e

Publication: PHENOMENES
SPATIAUX

Union des Groupement
Espiologiques de France (UGEF)
51 rue des Alpes
Valence (Drome), 26

Publication: CIEL INSOLITE

Publication (only): LUMIERES
DANS LA NUIT, Les Pins, 43 Le
Chambon-sur-Lignon

Germany

Deutsche UFO Studiengesellschaft
(DUIST)
62 Wiesbaden-Schierstein
Postfach 17185

Publication:
UFO NACHRICHTEN

Holland

Nederlands Onderzoek Bureau voor
Ongeeidentificeerde (NOBOVO)
Moleneind Z.z. 69
Drachten

Publication:
VLIEGENDE SCHOTEL
NIEUWS

Italy

Centro Unico Nazionale
Casella Postale 796
40100 Bologna

Publication: UFO NOTIZIARIO

Publication (only): CLYPEUS
Casella Postale 604
10100 Torino—Centro

Japan

Japan UFO Research Association
c/o Tomezo Hirata
2-2-7, Uozaki-Nakamachi
Higashi-Nadu-ku,
Kobe

Publication: JUFORA JOURNAL

New Zealand

Publication:
SPACEVIEW, P.O. Box 21007,
Henderson

Spain

Centro de Estudios Interplanetarios
(CEI)   (founded 1958)
Apartado Coreos 282
Barcelona

Publication: STENDEK

United Kingdom

British UFO Research Association
(BUFORA)   (founded 1962)
15 Freshwater Court
Crawford Street
London W1H 1HS

Publication: BUFORA JOURNAL

Publications (only):
FLYING SAUCER REVIEW
21 Cecil Court, London WC2

SPACELINK
15 Freshwater Court,
Crawford Street
London W1H 1HS

United States of America

Aerial Phenomena Research
Organisation (APRO)   (founded
1952)
3910 East Kleindale Road
Tucson
Arizona 85712

Publication: APRO BULLETIN

Midwest UFO Network (MUFON)
Box 129
Stover
Missouri 65078

Publication: SKYLOOK

National Investigations Committee
on Aerial Phenomena (NICAP)
Suite 801
1730 Rhode Island Avenue N.W.
Washington, D.C. 20036

Publication:
UFO INVESTIGATOR

Publication (only):
FLYING SAUCERS,
Amherst, Wisconsin 54406

List compiled by: Lionel Beer
                Vice-Chairman—British U.F.O. Research Association
                Publisher—SPACELINK

Lists of books and magazines for sale on UFO's and related subjects may be
obtained from: 15 Freshwater Court, Crawford Street, London W1H 1HS,
England.

STAY ON

Here are details of other exciting TARGET titles. If you cannot obtain these books from your local bookshop, or newsagent, write to the address below listing the titles you would like and enclosing cheque or postal order—*not* currency—including 15p per book to cover packing and postage; 2–4 books, 10p per copy; 5–8 books, 8p per copy.

TARGET BOOKS,
Universal-Tandem Publishing Co.,
14 Gloucester Road,
London SW7 4RD

INVESTIGATING GODS

Larry Kettelkamp

0 426 10268 1   **A Target Mystery**

Who am I? Have I lived before? What happens after death? Is there a God, or gods? How should I live this life? This book introduces young readers to the various ways in which man has attempted to explain his own existence, from the legend of Atlantis via the major religions to the present-day re-awakening of interest in the occult sciences. *Illustrated.*

THE STORY OF THE LOCH NESS MONSTER
Tim Dinsdale

0 426 10073 5   **A Target Mystery**

What mysterious entity lurks beneath the 1000 ft. deep, sinister-looking waters of Loch Ness in the Highlands of Scotland? Since the 1930s, men have sought the answer to this question. The author, a full-time, professional monster-hunter, tells you the history of the search for 'Nessie', and her cousin 'Morag', the monster of Loch Morar, and of the latest discoveries made with scientific equipment. *Fully illustrated with maps, photographs, and drawings.*

GHOSTS, GHOULS, AND OTHER HORRORS
Bernhardt J. Hurwood

0 426 10321 1   **A Target Mystery**

50 true, scarifying stories of the supernatural collected from Britain, Europe, America and other parts of the world. Shudder happily with these eerie tales of phantoms, headless apparitions, vampires and werewolves, and don't forget to turn the light out! *Illustrated.*

HAUNTED HOUSES
Bernhardt J. Hurwood

0 426 10559 1   **A Target Mystery**

Who was the ghost of Powis Castle? Why has he not been seen for 200 years? What was the cause of the fatal curse on Mouse Tower? And why does Anne Boleyn ride headless with a coach and four around the grounds of Blicking Hall? Here are 25 spine-chilling tales to spirit you away . . . into HAUNTED HOUSES! *Illustrated.*

COMMANDOS IN ACTION!
Graeme Cook

0 426 10508 7   **Target True-life Adventure**

True stories of Britain's immortal Commando Regiment—the crack military unit whose skill, determination and courage did so much to hamper Hitler's efforts to conquer this country during the Second World War. *Illustrated.*

DOCTOR WHO AND THE DAY OF THE DALEKS

Terrance Dicks

0 426 10380 7 **A Target Adventure**

Mysterious humans from 22nd century Earth 'time-jump' back into the 20th century so as to assassinate a high-ranking diplomat on whom the peace of the world depends. DOCTOR WHO, Jo Grant and the Brigadier are soon called in to investigate. Jo is accidentally transported forward to the 22nd century; the Doctor follows, eventually to be captured by his oldest and deadliest enemy, the DALEKS! Having submitted the Doctor to the fearful Mind Analysis Machine, the DALEKS plan a 'time-jump' attack on Earth in the 20th century! *Illustrated.*

DOCTOR WHO AND THE DOOMSDAY WEAPON

Malcolm Hulke

0 426 10372 6 **A Target Adventure**

The evil MASTER has stolen the Time Lords' file on the horrifying DOOMSDAY WEAPON with which, when he finds it, he can blast whole planets out of existence and make himself ruler of the Galaxy! The Time Lords direct DOCTOR WHO and Jo Grant in their TARDIS to a bleak planet in the year 2471 where they find colonists from Earth under threat from mysterious, savage, monster lizards with frightful claws! And hidden upon this planet is the DOOMSDAY WEAPON for which the MASTER is intently searching. *Illustrated.*

DOCTOR WHO AND THE DÆMONS

Barry Letts

0 426 10444 7 **A Target Adventure**

DOCTOR WHO is strangely concerned about Professor Horner's plan to cut open an ancient barrow near Devil's End; equally worried is Miss Hawthorne, the local white witch, who foretells a terrible disaster if he goes ahead; determined that he should is Mr. Magister, the new vicar (in truth the MASTER) whose secret ceremonies are designed to conjure up from out of the barrow a horribly powerful being from a far-off planet. An exciting adventure with the forces of black magic! *Illustrated.*

If you enjoyed this book and would like to have information sent you about other TARGET titles, write to the address below.

You will also receive:
A FREE TARGET BADGE!
Based on the TARGET BOOKS symbol—see front cover of this book—this attractive three-colour badge, pinned to your blazer-lapel or jumper, will excite the interest and comment of all your friends!

and you will be further entitled to:
FREE ENTRY INTO THE TARGET DRAW!
All you have to do is cut off the coupon beneath, write on it your name and address in *block capitals*, and pin it to your letter. Twice a year, in June and December, coupons will be drawn 'from the hat' and the winner will receive a complete year's set of TARGET books.

Write to:

TARGET BOOKS,
Universal-Tandem
Publishing Co.
14, Gloucester Road,
London SW7 4RD

If you live in South Africa,
write to:

TARGET BOOKS,
Purnell & Sons,
505, C.N.A. Building,
110, Commissioner Street,
Johannesburg

If you live in New Zealand,
write to:

TARGET BOOKS,
Whitcoulls Ltd.,
111, Cashel Street,
Christchurch

If you live in Australia,
write to:

TARGET BOOKS,
Rical Enterprises Pty. Ltd.,
Daking House,
11, Rawson Place,
Sydney, N.S. Wales 2000

———————————— cut here ————————————

Full name..

Address..

....

....

Age................................

PLEASE ENCLOSE A SELF-ADDRESSED ENVELOPE WITH YOUR COUPON.